ITALIAN

BY HOWARD TOMB

WORKMAN PUBLISHING · NEW YORK

ACKNOWLEDGMENTS

Many thanks to Ilaria Lemme and her family, Patty
Brown, John Boswell, Michael Cader, Sally
Kovalchick, Carol McKeown, and Ben Stoner.

Library of Congress Cataloging-in-Publication Data
Tomb, Howard, 1959–
    Wicked Italian.

    1. Italian language—Conversation and phrase
books—Humor. 2. Italy—Description and
travel—1975—Guide-books—Humor. 3. Voyages and
travels—Humor. I. Title.
PN6231.I84T66   1989   458.3'421   88-40247
ISBN 0-89480-617-3

Illustrations by Jared Lee
Cover and book design by Paul Hanson

Workman books are available at special discounts when
purchased in bulk for premiums and sales promotions as
well as for fund-raising or educational use. Special editions
or book excerpts can also be created to specification. For details,
contact the Special Sales Director at the address below.

Workman Publishing, 708 Broadway, New York, NY 10003

Manufactured in the United States of America
First printing June 1989

20 19 18 17

CONTENTS

WELCOME TO ITALY

Italians will love you in the same way they love a good *prosciutto:* They will admire your color and your firm, lightly marbled flesh. They may even revel in your aroma. Then they will devour you.

And even before the last morsels of your body and soul have been consumed, they'll be thinking about the next course.

If being torn to pieces and eaten alive sounds like the perfect vacation experience, this book will help you choose exactly whose menu you end up on.

If you prefer instead to see a few museums and do a little shopping, this book will help you stay out of the slaughterhouse altogether.

Wicked Italian is meant to transform you into a complete traveler, capable of subtle understanding, intelligent discourse, and effective verbal assault.

HAND-TO-HAND CONVERSATION

In order to have the slightest chance of making yourself understood in Italy, you need to take a little care in pronunciation, and use a few basic hand motions. Gestures clarify the underlying meaning of Italian phrases.

The most popular gesture is made with the fingertips of one hand drawn together, chest high, pointing skyward, while the hand makes little bouncing motions. This gesture adds emphasis to any statement or question, such as *"Ma che sei scemo!"* (You nitwit!) and *"Grazie mille per aver rovesciato il sugo sulla mia cravatta nuova"* (Thank you very much for spilling sauce on my new tie.) Two hands are twice as emphatic as one.

One of the most famous Italian gestures, biting the middle knuckle of the index finger, means either a) *Ti spezzerei in due"* (I'll break you in half) or b) *"Sei troppo sexy; non lo sopporto"* (You're too sexy; I can't stand it).

Italians have a gesture that replaces the relatively unwieldy British phrase "wink, wink, nudge, nudge, say no more." It can also be taken to mean "very clever." The index finger is placed just below the eye, touching the cheek, pulling the lower eyelid down ever so slightly. *"Ci capiamo, eh?"* (We understand each other, eh?)

The key dinner-table gesture has the index

finger pointing into the cheek like a pistol, turning back and forth. The eyes are rolled toward heaven. *"Che cuoca!"* (What a chef!)

Every traveler needs a gesture to express general disdain. In Italy, the lower lip is extended. A flat hand is held horizontally with the palm downward and brushed against the chin as if feeling whiskers. *"Non me ne importa un accidente."* (I don't give a darn.)

Now, if you can roll your *r*'s, you're ready to begin. *Buona fortuna!*

LINGUISTIC DISCLAIMER

Because the Italian language is one of complex diction, pronunciation, and gesticulation, no book can prepare readers for every eventuality or even convey foolproof phonetic information to the typical tone-deaf tourist.

Therefore, the author and his publisher, editors, translators, agents, attorneys, bodyguards, and heirs must hereby deny and firmly push away from their persons all responsibility for any intercultural misunderstandings that result in embarrassing errors or gaffes, unintended insults, wild accusations, fisticuffs, general riot, total war, or anchovies.

CLASSIC BORDER PLEAS

The Italian frontier is fairly porous; innocent people entering the country may not even see an *agente di dogana* (customs agent). Visitors who carry *contrabbando*, however, are usually met at the airport by some heavily armed soldiers and their large carnivorous dogs.

I was not at my best when the photo was taken.	*Non ero molto in forma quando ho fatto la foto.*	*Noan AIR-oh MOLE-toh een FORM-ah KWAN-doh oh FAH-toh lah FOH-toh.*
I have nothing to declare.	*Non ho nulla da dichiarare.*	*Noan oh NOOL-ah dah DEE-kyah-RAR-ay.*
Well, not much, anyway. Nice doggie!	*Beh, non molto. Bel cagnolino!*	*Beh, noan MOLE-toh. Bell CON-yoh-LEAN-oh!*
I don't think you want to look in there.	*Non credo che lei voglia guardare anche lì dentro.*	*Noan CRAY-doh kay lay VOLE-yah gwar-DAR-ay ONK-ay lee DEN-troh.*
I've never seen that before.	*Non ho mai visto quella cosa prima d'ora.*	*Noan oh my VEEST-oh KWELL-ah COZE-ah PREE-mah DORE-ah.*

Ah ha! This isn't my bag!	*Ah ah! Questa non è la mia valigia!*	*Ah ah! KWEST-ah noan ay lah MEE-ah vah-LEE-jah!*
I'm sorry, but strip searches are against my religion.	*Spiacente, ma le perquisizioni sono contrarie alla mia religione.*	*SPEE-ah-CHENT-ay, mah lay pair-KWEEZ-eats-ee-OWN-ay SO-noh cone-TRAR-ee-ay AH-lah MEE-ah ray-lee-JOAN-ay.*
What's that rubber glove/flashlight for?	*A cosa serve quel guanto di gomma/lampada?*	*Ah COZE-ah SAIR-vay kwell GWON-toh dee GOME-ah/lomm-POD-ah?*
Wait. I'll confess.	*Aspetti. Confesso.*	*Ah-SPETT-ee. Cone-FESS-oh.*

THE PRACTICAL TRAVELER

ENDING TAXI TERROR

Frequent travelers to Italy are familiar with the symptoms of Taxi Terror: feverish prayer, piercing screams, loose bowels, and cardiac arrest.

But there is hope. Every taxi ride doesn't have to feel like your last. Brace yourself, close your eyes, and repeat these phrases to yourself:

"This driver is a professional."

"This driver knows the exact width of his car."

"This driver is accurate to within millimeters, even at high speeds."

"This driver carries full liability insurance."

If your vehicular hysteria is not soothed by these mantras, or you think you're being cheated on the fare, repeat these phrases to the driver.

Please slow down.	*Rallenti, per favore.*	*Rah-LENT-ee, pair fah-VORE-ay.*
I'd like to go to the train station, not into orbit.	*Vorrei andare alla stazione, non vada in orbita.*	*Vore-AY on-DAR-ay AH-lah STOT-zee-OWN-ay, noan VAH-dah in ORB-eet-ah.*
Sir, if you truly have a death wish, I'll be happy to oblige you.	*Signore, se veramente vuole morire, l'accontento.*	*Seen-YORE-ay, say VAIR-ah-MENT-ay VWO-lay moh-REE-ray, lah-cone-TENT-oh.*

So this is the new Italian fighter jet!	*Quindi, questo è il nuovo aereo da combattimento italiano!*	*KWEEN-dee, KWEST-oh ay eel NWOH-voh ah-AIR-ay-oh coam-BAT-ee-MENT-oh ee-tal-YON-oh.*
Ingenious camouflage!	*Ingegnosa mimitizzazione!*	*Een-jen-YOH-sah mee-mee-teet-ZOT-zee-OWN-ay!*
If you don't slow down, I'll barf.	*Se non rallenta, vomito.*	*Say noan rah-LENT-ah, VOME-eet-oh.*

UNDERSTANDING YOUR FARE

The amount shown on an Italian taxi meter is often well below the price quoted by the driver. His calculation is based upon a formula rumored to be the metered fare multiplied by $p^2 + h/2 + t + (s - 10k)/x$, where p represents the number of passengers, h the number of bags, t the number of hours past 8:00 P.M., s the cost of your shoes in lire, k your weight in kilograms, and x anything he damn well pleases. Some negotiation is possible, but most drivers expect to get the fare they state, up to fifty percent beyond what's on the meter.

DOING THE LOCOMOTION

Men who hope to meet Italian women on trains will need more than body language. They'll also need semiplausible opening lines, silky voices, and expensive cologne. Armed with these accoutrements, Englishmen and Americans have a slight advantage over their Italian counterparts: We are thought to be more sincere.

Traditional railway seduction begins with a long conversation.

Pardon me. Could you recommend any vineyards or restaurants in Tuscany?	*Scusi, può indicarmi qualche vigna o ristorante in Toscana?*	*SKOO-see, pwoh EEN-dee-CAR-mee KWALL-kay VEEN-yah oh REEST-oh-RONT-ay een toe-SKAH-nah?*
How did Milan surpass Paris as the capital of fashion and cuisine?	*Com'è che Milano ha superato Parigi ed è diventata la capitale della moda e della cucina?*	*Coh-MAY kay mee-LON-oh ah SOOP-air-OT-oh pah-REE-jee ed ay DEE-ven-TOT-ah lah COP-ee-TAL-ay DELL-ah MODE-ah ay DELL-ah coo-CHEEN-ah?*
Tell me about Garibaldi.	*Mi racconti di Garibaldi.*	*Mee rah-CONE-tee dee gar-ee-BALD-ee.*

What role does the Catholic church play in the Italy of today?	*Che ruolo ha la chiesa Cattolica in Italia oggi?*	*Kay ru-OLE-oh ah la key-AZE-ah cah-TOLE-ee-cah een ee-TAL-ya OH-jee?*
How unfaithful are Italian men, really?	*Quanto sono infedeli, in realtà, gli uomini italiani?*	*KWON-toh SO-noh EEN-fee-DAY-lee, een ray-AL-ee-TAH, lyee WHOA-mee-nee ee-tal-YON-ee?*

NOTE TO MEN

Avoid sitting near, speaking to, or looking at the mother, sister, wife, daughter, niece, or nanny of any successful Sicilian businessman or of any such businessman's personal friend. Do not even *think* of such a man's granddaughter.

THE PRACTICAL TRAVELER 🧳

TRAIN TRAVEL TIPS

Italians have an optimistic way of describing trains. The *diretto* and *accelerato* are local trains, which stop not only at every station but also between stations.

Each time the train stops, more people get on, and fresh arguments take place as to who has reserved what seat. Therefore, nonstop trains should be taken whenever possible. These are the *espresso* and the *rapido*, the real express trains.

The *bigliettaio* (ticket collector) and *ferroviere* (conductor) will be only too happy to help you enjoy and understand your train ride. For a small tip they might even kick somebody out of your seat.

Once you've settled into your compartment, you may find that trains are a great place to get in touch with Italians, whether you want to or not.

THROWING THE SWITCH

People who want to avoid getting to know their fellow train travelers need a few pointed phrases either to stop conversations in their tracks or derail them completely.

Do you do your own tailoring?	*Fa i suoi vestiti da solo?*	*Fah ee swoy ves-TEET-ee dah solo?*
And you cut your own hair, too?	*E taglia anche i suoi capelli?*	*Ay TALL-ya ONK-ay ee swoy cah-PELL-ee?*
Have you accepted Jesus Christ as your personal savior?	*Lei ha accettato Gesù Cristo come il suo salvatore?*	*Lay ah AH-chay-TOT-oh jay-ZOO CREEST-oh COH-may eel SOO-oh SAL-vah-TORE-ay?*
Want to see a really big boil?	*Vorrebbe vedere un vero e proprio foruncolone?*	*Vore-ABE-ay vay-DARE-ay oon VAIR-oh ay PRO-pree-oh for-OON-coh-LOH-nay?*
Let's discuss your insurance needs.	*Parliamo della sua assicuzazioni.*	*Par-lee-YAH-mo DELL-ah SOO-ah ah-seh-coo-zah-zee-OH-nee.*

THE PRACTICAL TRAVELER 🧳

YOU CAN WIN AT HOTEL NEGOTIATION

An unscrupulous hotel manager may attempt to palm off an inferior room on unsuspecting tourists, or to extract a *mancia* (literally, tip; actually, bribe) in exchange for a room by insisting that the hotel is full.

We made these reservations six months ago.	*Abbiamo riservato sei mesi fa.*	*Ah-bee-OM-oh REE-zare-VOT-oh SAY MAY-zee fah.*
Then we will sleep here in the lobby.	*Allora dormiamo nella lobby.*	*Ah-LORE-ah DOR-mee-YOM-oh NELL-ah LOBE-ee.*
We reserved a room with a view.	*Avevamo riservato una camera con vista.*	*AH-vay-VOM-oh REE-zare-VOT-oh OON-ah COM-air-ah cone VEEST-ah.*
The sheets are still damp.	*Le lenzuola sono ancora umide.*	*Lay lens-WHOA-la SO-noh on-CORE-ah OOM-ee-day.*
What is that smell?	*Cos'è quell'odore?*	*Coze-AY kwell-oh-DORE-ay?*
Something is living in the bathroom.	*C'è qualcosa nel bagno.*	*Chay kwall-COZE-ah nell BON-ya*

There is no hot water. The cold water is brown.	*Non c'è acqua calda. L'acqua fredda è marrone.*	*Noan chay OCK-wah CALD-ah. LOCK-wah FRAID-ah ay mah-RONE-ay.*
Is this a towel or a postage stamp?	*È un asciugamano o un francobollo?*	*Ay oon ah-SHOOG-ah-MON-oh oh oon FRONK-oh-BOWL-oh?*
Four stars my ass! More like four dogs, I'd say!	*Quattro stelle un accidente! Direi quattro cani, invece!*	*KWAH-troh STELL-ay oon OTCH-ee-DENT-ay! Dee-RAY KWAH-troh CON-ee, een-VAY-chay!*
Get me a taxi.	*Mi chiami un taxi.*	*Me KYAH-mee oon taxi.*
This is a much better room. Thank you.	*Questa stanza va molto meglio. Grazie.*	*KWEST-ah STON-zah vah MOLE-toh MAIL-yoh. GROT-zee-ay.*
Here's something for your trouble.	*Questo per il disturbo.*	*KWEST-oh pair eel dee-STAIR-boh.*

THE PRACTICAL TRAVELER 💼

FENDING OFF GYPSY CURSES

Because of its proximity to Eastern Europe, Italy has more than its share of the permanent tourists known as Gypsies. If you don't give a *zingara* (Gypsy woman) money on demand, she will curse your entire family, your rental car, your stockbroker, and your reproductive organs. Then her children will pick your pockets.

They usually work in pairs: One slobbers on you, eyes crossed, while the other rummages through your clothing for valuables and unusual postcards.

The threat of a *schiaffo* (slap) may be enough to disperse the urchins, but phrases are provided just in case.

I haven't any coins.	*Non ho soldi spiccioli.*	*Noan oh SOLE-dee SPEECH-oh-li.*
Now get lost.	*Allora, vattene.*	*Ah-LORE-ah, VAH-tay-nay.*
On your mother's grave!	*Sulla tomba di tua madre!*	*SOO-lah TOME-bah dee TOO-ah MAH-dray!*
And may the rest of your teeth rot before Christmas!	*E possano i tuoi denti marcire prima di Natale!*	*Ay POE-sah-noh ee twoy DENT-ee mar-CHEER-ay PREE-mah dee nah-TAL-ay!*

Okay, here's fifty cents.	*OK, ecco cinquecento lire.*	*Oh kay, EK-oh CHEEN-kway-CHENT-oh LEER-ay.*
Now, leave us alone.	*Allora, lasciaci in pace.*	*Ah-LORE-ah, LOSH-ah-chee in PAH-chay.*
Stop thief!	*Al ladro!*	*Ahl LAH-droh!*
Arrest these children.	*Arresti questi bambini.*	*Ah-REST-ee KWEST-ee bam-BEAN-ee.*

A ROSE IS A RUSE

Many Gypsies sell single red roses wrapped in plastic. Travelers with foresight will buy one of these mummified blooms on Day One. The rose can be kept indefinitely in a pocket or purse for display when flower sellers appear.

THE PRACTICAL TRAVELER 🧳

THE ITALIAN PHONE SYSTEM

Italian phones are scarce and unreliable. Callers must dial slowly, but not too slowly, spacing the numbers evenly. Long-distance rates are simple: Each thirty-minute call costs as much as first-class airfare to the same location.

Operator? I'd like to call New York.	*Centralinista? Vorrei chiamare New York.*	*Chentrah-lee-NEEST-ah? Vore-AY kyah-MAR-ay new york.*
Please speak more slowly.	*Parli più lentamente, per favore.*	*PAR-lee pyu LENT-ah-MENT-ay, pair fah-VORE-ay.*
Could I have an English-speaking operator?	*Può passarmi un centralinista che parli inglese?*	*Pwoh poss-ARE-me oon chentrah-lee-NEEST-ah kay PAR-lee een-GLAZE-ay?*
Are you speaking English now?	*Parla inglese allora?*	*PAR-lah een-GLAZE-ay ah-LORE-ah?*
How long will it take to get through?	*Quanto ci vorrà per avere la comunicazione?*	*KWON-toh chee vore-AH pair ah-VAIR-ay la coh-MOON-ee-COT-zee-OWN-ay?*

I can wait for only four days.	*Posso aspettare solo quattro giorni.*	*POE-soh ah-spet-TAR-ay solo KWAH-troh JOR-nee.*
How much will that cost?	*Quanto verrà a costare?*	*KWON-toh vair-AH ah coast-AR-ay?*
Make that a collect call, please.	*A spese ricevente, per favore.*	*Ah SPAZE-ay reech-ay-VENT-ay, pair fah-VORE-ay.*

PRAYER TO SAINT ILARIA, VIRGIN OF NAPLES

Holy virgin Ilaria, Your Revered Pureness, Only Virgin of Naples, allow me to get his/her phone number, the blonde one by the bar. I swear that my intentions are entirely honorable, Your Stubbornness. Amen.

Santa Ilaria Vergine, Sua Venerata Purezza, Unica Vergine di Napoli, aiutami ad avere il numero di telefono del biondo/della bionda del bar. Giuro che le mie intenzioni sono più che serie, Sua Ostinazione. Amen.

THE PRACTICAL TRAVELER 🧳

ITALIAN DRUGS YOU MAY NEED

Drugs are the only answer to some travel disasters. In order to get the right *medicina* (drug), one must know brand names and their pronunciations.

DISASTER	DRUG OF CHOICE	NOTE
Headache	*Novalgina (NO-vall-JEEN-ah)*	*Liquid analgesic; not supposed to upset stomach.*
Overeating	*Diger Seltz (DEE-jair seltz)*	*Might as well buy the twelve-pack.*
Sleeplessness	*Mogadon (MOAG-ah-DOAN)*	*Probably not strong enough to overcome Italian espresso*
Constipation	*Guttalax (GOOT-ah-LOX)*	*The amount of olive oil in the Italian diet should render this drug unnecessary.*

HOW AND WHEN TO QUOTE DANTE

Dante Alighieri was not your average Florentine poet. He was and is Italy's Shakespeare.

Natives will be flattered by non-Italian visitors who quote Dante. But quoting *il poeta della Divina Commedia* (the poet of the *Divine Comedy*) at length is considered pompous. Better to drop a few lines in appropriate situations.

At the station entrance during a general strike:

Abandon all hope, ye who enter here.	*Lasciate ogni speranza, voi che entrate.*	*Losh-AH-tay OWN-yee spare-ON-za, voy kay en-TROT-ay.*

After a really huge helping of *pasta al pesto:*

There is no greater ache than to remember the happy times in misery.	*Non c'è nessun maggior dolore che ricordarsi del tempo felice nella miseria.*	*Noan chay nay-SOON mah-JORE doh-LOAR-ay kay RE-core-DAR-see dell TEMP-oh fay-LEECH-ay NELL-ah mee-ZAIR-ee-ah.*

At a passing busload of tourists tackier than thou:

O foolish creatures, what ignorance is this which torments you?	*O creature sciocche, quanta ignoranza è quella che v'offende?*	*Oh crayah-TURE-ay SHOKE-ay, KWON-tah EEN-yore-ONZ-ah ay KWELL-ah kay voh-FEND-ay?*

ELEMENTARY CURSING

Italian is a sharp, crisp language, and Mediterranean tempers are hot. As a result, Italians enjoy a special expertise in cursing.

Hurting someone's feelings is plenty of fun until he breaks your legs. As with all curses, these are best used when the subject is well out of earshot.

Turd.	*Stronzo.*	*STRONE-zo*
Cretin.	*Cretino.*	*Cray-TEEN-oh.*
Wimp (human larva).	*Larva umana.*	*LAR-vah oo-MON-ah.*
He is a worm.	*Lui è un verme.*	*LOO-ee ay oon VAIR-may.*
She's brainless.	*Lei è senza cervello.*	*Lay ay SEN-sah chair-VELL-oh.*
They are all bad eggs.	*Son tutte uova marce.*	*Soan TOOT-ay WHOA-vah MAR-chay.*
Screw yourself.	*Vaffanculo.*	*VA-fon-COOL-oh.*
You have no class (literally, "You're a dockworker").	*Lei è uno scaricatore di porto.*	*LAY ay OON-oh SCAR-ee-cah-TORE-ay dee PORT-oh.*

■ THE PRACTICAL TRAVELER

An utter scoundrel, and ugly, too.	*Un perfetto mascalzone e anche brutto.*	*Oon pair-FETT-oh MAH-scal-ZONE-ay ay ONK-ay BRUTE-oh.*
Complete asshole.	*Proprio uno stronzo.*	*PRO-pree-oh OON-oh STRONE-zo*
Filthy parasite.	*Sporco parassita.*	*SPORE-coh PAR-ah-SEET-ah.*
Hateful fool.	*Odioso zuccone.*	*OH-dee-OH-soh zoo-CONE-ay.*
Your father is as smart as a chicken.	*Tuo padre è un pollo.*	*TOO-oh PAH-dray ay oon POLE-oh.*
May your children have the faces of baboons.	*Ti possano venire dei figli con la faccia da babbuini.*	*Tee POE-son-oh ven-EER-ay day FEEL-yee cone lah FOTCH-ah dah BOB-oo-EEN-ee.*

DRIVE AND SURVIVE

THE AUTOMOBILE: AN ITALIAN LOVE AFFAIR

Because gas is so expensive, few Italians can afford to drive Ferraris, Lamborghinis, or the larger Maseratis. Instead, they endow their Fiats and Alfas with features more common on exotic cars, such as delicate fuel-injection systems and impossible-to-find parts.

Travelers who plan to drive in Italy should learn a little authentic car talk in order to speak to service-station employees and mechanics.

Fill it up, please.	*Il pieno, per favore.*	*Eel pee-AY-noh, pair fah-VORE-ay.*
Premium. I need that extra horsepower.	*Super. Ho bisogno di più potenza.*	*SOOP-air. Oh bee-ZONE-yoh dee pyu poh-TENZ-ah.*
Only sixty-five dollars? Hell of a deal.	*Soltanto ottanta mila? Che buon'affare.*	*Sole-TONT-oh oh-TONT-ah MEAL-ah? Kay bwone ah-FAR-ay.*
Oh my God! What's that sickening sound?	*Oh mio Dio! Cos'è quell'orribile rumore?*	*Oh MEE-oh DEE-oh! Coze-AY kwell ore-EEB-ee-lay roo-MORE-ay?*

🚗 *DRIVE AND SURVIVE*

Perhaps it's the transmission/ engine/exhaust.	*Forse è il cambio/motore/ tubo di scappamento.*	*FOR-say ay eel COM-bee-oh/ moh-TORE-ay/ TOO-bo dee SCAH-pah-MENT-oh.*
Can it be fixed? How long will it take?	*Si può riparare? Quanto ci vorrà?*	*See pwoh ree-par-ARE-ay? KWON-toh chee vore-AH?*
Where may we buy train tickets?	*Dove possiamo comprare dei biglietti del treno?*	*DOH-vay POE-see-OM-oh coam-PRAR-ay day beel-YET-ee dell TRAIN-oh?*

PRAYER TO SAINT LAURA OF ROME

Saint Laura, Princess of Meter Maids, Mother of Tiny Cars, please provide us with a legal parking place in Trastevere this Saturday night. Two hours is all we ask, Your Holy Bureaucracy.

Santa Laura, Principessa delle Vigilesse, Madre delle Piccole Auto, ti preghiamo di aiutarci affinché possiamo trovare un parcheggio a Trastevere questo sabato sera. Due ore è tutto ciò che chiediamo, Sua Santa Burocrazia.

DRIVE AND SURVIVE 🚗

LYING TO POLICEMEN: THE NATIONAL PASTIME

The stupidity of *carabinieri*, the Italian military police, is so legendary that a garden slug would be embarrassed to join their ranks.

No one knows how the military finds replacements for the hundreds of officers who annually shoot themselves with pistols they thought weren't loaded, set their pants on fire, and drive off cliffs in broad daylight. Yet fresh *carabinieri* are found, ready for long hours, low pay, and the scorn of an entire nation.

Is there a problem, officer?	*C'è qualcosa che non va, agente?*	*Chay kwall-COZE-ah kay noan vah, ah-JENT-ay?*
I thought the light was green.	*Mi sembrava che il semaforo fosse verde.*	*Mee sem-BRAH-vah kay eel same-AH-fore-oh FOSS-ay VAIR-day.*
A one-way street? Is that so!	*Senso unico? Davvero!*	*SEN-soh OON-ee-coh? Dah-VAIR-oh!*
I am truly sorry.	*Mi dispiace davvero.*	*Mee DEE-spee-YOTCH-ay dah-VAIR-oh.*

But to tell you the truth, I wasn't behind the wheel.	*Ma a dire il vero, non stavo guidando io.*	*Mah ah DEER-ay eel VAIR-oh, noan STAH-voh gwee-DON-doh EE-oh.*
That was my twin brother/sister.	*Quello/a era il mio gemello/la mia gemella.*	*KWELL-oh/-ah AIR-ah eel MEE-oh jay-MELL-oh/ lah MEE-ah jay-MELL-ah.*
He's/She's out of town this week.	*È fuori città questa settimana.*	*Ay FWOR-ee chee-TAH KWEST-ah SET-ee-MON-ah.*
I'll have him/her call you when he/she returns.	*La farò chiamare quando ritorna.*	*La far-OH kyah-MAR-ay KWON-doh ree-TORN-ah.*
Yes, of course. I'll tell him/her to drive more carefully.	*Sì, naturalmente. Gli/Le dirò di guidare più prudentemente.*	*See, NOT-ur-ahl-MENT-ay. Lyee/ Lay deer-OH dee gwee-DAR-ay pyu pru-DENT-eh-MENT-ay.*

DRIVE AND SURVIVE 🚗

ASSORTED INTERNATIONAL SYMBOLS

All motorists must learn to decipher basic road signs. But there are many obscure international symbols that alert the astute driver to cultural hazards and opportunities.

PICTURESQUE
OLD MEN
AHEAD

SAINT'S TEETH
NEXT LEFT

OUTRAGEOUS
PRICES
NEXT 20 KM

VIRGIN
500 METERS

WARNING:
HORNY MEN
NEXT 10 KM

SHOUTING IN TRAFFIC

An *epiteto* (epithet) is satisfying only if the intended victim understands it. Visiting drivers may start their own authentic Italian shouting matches with these phrases.

(Note: Italian tempers are not just the stuff of legend; they are real. Before using these lines, lock the doors and put your vehicle in gear.)

What a jerk!	*Che pezzo di stupido!*	*Kay PET-zoh dee STOO-pee-doh!*
What are you? Crazy?	*Ma è pazzo?*	*Mah ay POT-soh?*
Move that junk pile, you cretin!	*Muova quel rottame, cretino!*	*Moo-OH-vah kwell roh-TOM-ay, cray-TEEN-oh!*
You drive like a ninety-year-old woman!	*Guida come una novantenne!*	*GWEE-dah COH-may OON-ah NO-von-TEN-ay!*
Have you swallowed your brain?	*Ti sei bevuto il cervello?*	*Tee say bay-VOOT-oh eel chair-VELL-oh?*
Maybe they will teach you to drive in hell.	*Speriamo che all'inferno le insegnino a guidare.*	*SPARE-ee-YOM-oh kay ahl-in-FAIRN-oh lay in-SANE-yair-ON-oh ah gwee-DAR-ay.*

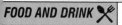

BEAUTIFUL NAMES OF REVOLTING DISHES AND VICE VERSA

Italian chefs have some unattractive names for wonderful dishes. *Pasta alla puttanesca*, for example, means "spaghetti of the slut," so called because it doesn't require hours in the kitchen. *Saltimbocca*, a classic Roman dish that translates as "jump in the mouth," is sliced veal with Marsala, ham, and sage. *Zuppa dei poveri*, "soup of the poor," is a hearty mixture of greens, oil, cheese, and stale bread.

Just as great dishes may have unfortunate names, revolting dishes may sound delicious. Even astute travelers can be fooled. Those with delicate sensibilities should take note of the following phrases, in order to recognize and decline alien entrées. (Euphemism has been eliminated in the English phrases.)

Please cut the head off.	*Per piacere, mi tagli quella testa.*	*Pair pee-ah-CHAIR-ay, mee TAL-yee KWELL-ah TASTE-ah.*
Thank you, but I had blood pudding for breakfast.	*Grazie, ma ho già avuto una torta al sangue per prima colazione.*	*GROT-zee-ay, mah oh jah ah-VOOT-oh OON-ah TORT-ah al SAHN-gway pair PREE-mah coh-LATS-ee-OWN- ay.*

I'm violently allergic to pickled eels.	*Sono davvero allergico/a alle anguille sotto aceto.*	*SO-noh da-VAIR-oh ah-LAIR-jee-coh/cah AH-lay on-GWEEL-ay SOTE-oh ah-CHET-oh.*
Also to stewed frogs and reptiles of any kind.	*Ed anche agli stufati di rane e rettili di ogni genere.*	*Aid ONK-ay AHL-yee stoo-FOT-ee dee RAH-nay ay RAY-tee-lee dee OWN-yee JEN-air-ay.*
The rabbit smothered in bitter chocolate sounds a bit heavy.	*La lepre piemontese mi risulta un po' pesante.*	*Lah LEP-ray PEE-moan-TAZE-ay mee ree-SOOLT-ah oon poe pay-ZONT-ay.*
Excuse me, but which organs are these?	*Scusi, ma che organi sono questi?*	*SKOO-see, mah kay OR-gan-ee SO-noh KWEST-ee?*
You're out of grilled lamb's guts?	*Non ha più nessuna cordula?*	*Noan ah pyu nay-SOON-ah core-DOOL-ah?*
What a pity! Perhaps the brains with capers, then.	*Che peccato! Allora, cervella con i capperi.*	*Kay pay-COT-oh! Ah-LORE-ah, chair-VELL-ah cone ee ca-PAIR-ay.*

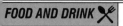

FOOD AND DRINK

DECLINING THE IMPERATIVE

Italian cooks may be genuinely hurt when guests cannot eat everything they serve. They don't realize that people in other civilizations consume less than their own weight at mealtime.

When you've had your fill, you can help a cook preserve her respect for you and for herself with a few carefully chosen phrases.

This is the best food I have ever tasted in my life.	*Questo è il miglior cibo che abbia mai assaggiato.*	*KWEST-oh ay eel MEAL-yore CHEE-boh kay AH-bee-yah my ah-sah-JAH-toh.*
I am your slave.	*Sono il tuo schiavo.*	*SO-noh eel TOO-oh ski-OV-oh.*
This meal has given me metric tons of joy, but I'm stuffed to the gills.	*Questo pasto mi ha dato mille tonnellate di gioia, ma sono pieno fin sopra la testa.*	*KWEST-oh PAH-stoh me ah DOT-oh MEAL-ay TONE-el-AH-tay dee JOY-ah, ma SO-noh pee-EN-oh feen SOAP-rah la TASTE-ah.*
Please. No more food. Thank you.	*Per favore. Non datemi nient'altro da mangiare. Grazie.*	*Pair fah-VORE-ay. Noan DOT-ay-me nee-EN-TAL-troh da mon-JAR-ay. GROT-zee-ay.*

SECRETS OF THE ITALIAN COFFEE SHOP

Prices in a *bar,* or coffee shop, differ depending on the customer's posture and geographical location. Plumbing the mysteries of this pricing system requires four simple questions.

How much is coffee standing up?	*Quanto è il caffè al banco?*	*KWON-toh ay eel cah-FAY all BONK-oh?*
How much if I sit here by the bar?	*Quanto è al tavolino?*	*KWON-toh ay all TAH-voh-LEEN-oh?*
How much seated on the terrace?	*È quanto sulla terrazza?*	*Ay KWON-toh SOOL-ah tare-OTZ-ah?*
How much in the restaurant next door?	*È quanto al ristorante accanto?*	*Ay KWON-toh all REEST-oh-RONT-ay ah CON-toh?*

MEANINGFUL THINGS TO SAY ABOUT OLIVE OIL

Good Italian olive oil is so delicious that philosophers have cited it as proof of the existence of God. Italians take olive oil as seriously as the French do wine, and an ability to comment on olive oil is a sign of sophistication in the traveler.

This olive oil has a subtle, sweet virginity.	*Questo olio d'oliva è di una verginità molto sottile, molto dolce.*	*KWEST-oh OH-leo doe-LEE-vah ay dee OON-ah vair-JEEN-ee-TAH MOLE-toh soh-TEEL-ay, MOLE-toh DOLE-chay.*
One taste tells you the olives grew in full view of the cathedral.	*Un assaggio ti dice che le olive sono maturate di fronte ad una cattedrale.*	*Oon ah-SAH-joe tee DEE-chay kay lay oh-LEE-vay SO-noh MAH-too-ROT-ay dee FRONE-tay ad OON-ah COT-ay-DRAHL-ay.*
They were hand-picked by the Blind Nuns of Tuscany.	*Sono state raccolte dalle suore cieche della Toscana.*	*SO-noh STAH-tay rah-COLT-ay DAH-lay SWORE-ay CHECK-ay DELL-ah toe-SKAH-nah.*

And cold-pressed just before puberty.	*Sono state spremute appena prima della pubertà.*	*So-noh STAH-tay spray-MOOT-ay ah-PAIN-ah PREE-mah DELL-ah POO-bare-TAH.*
Just wait until you taste the extra virgin!	*Ma aspetta di assaggiare quello extra vergine!*	*Mah ah-SPETT-ah-dee AH-sah-JAR-ay KWELL-oh EX-trah VAIR-jeen-ay.*

YOUR INEVITABLE STAINS

Every restaurant in Italy stocks a bottle of *borotalco* (unscented talc) with which to dust olive oil stains. Seasoned travelers can tell what a person had for dinner according to the size, shape, and location of his or her talc marks. Long pastas such as spaghetti can fling oil for several feet, leaving welt-like marks from collar to cuff. Short pastas tend to drop and stick, leaving their unmistakeable impressions on and about the thigh region. Slippery, round pastas such as rigatoni tend to drop and roll, leaving the ever-popular *linea incisa* (hatch mark) and classic *ellissi* (ellipses).

YOUR MEDICAL EMERGENCY

Explaining ailments to foreign doctors is never easy, and covering all medical terminology is beyond the scope of this book. Phrases are provided for a restaurant setting, where Italian medical emergencies are most likely to occur.

Is there a doctor in the house?	*C'è un dottore in casa?*	*Chay oon doe-TORE-ay een CAH-zah?*
I don't know what's wrong.	*Non capisco cos'è che non và.*	*Noan cah-PEACE-coh coze-AY kay noan vah.*
He started drinking the olive oil straight.	*Lui si è attaccato alla bottiglia dell'olio d'oliva.*	*LOO-ee see ay at-ah-COT-oh AH-lah boh-TEEL-yah dell-OH-leo doe-LEE-vah.*
Then he fell over unconscious.	*Poi ha perso i sensi.*	*Poy ah PAIR-soh ee SEN-see.*
Yes, it certainly is good oil. Extra virgin.	*Si, è certamente un buon olio. Extra vergine.*	*See, ay CHAIR-tah-MENT-ay oon bwone OH-leo EX-trah VAIR-jeen-ay.*
I'm happy to hear you think he'll recover.	*Mi fa piacere sentire che si rimetterà.*	*Me fah pee-ah-CHAIR-ay sen-TEAR-ay kay see rim-ET-air-AH.*

When should I remove the leeches?	*Quando posso rimuovere le sanguisughe?*	*KWON-doh POE-soh ree-MWOH-vair-ay lay sahng-gwee-SOOG-ay?*
I'm afraid I don't have that much cash at the moment.	*Mi dispiace, ma al momento non ho tutto questo contante.*	*Me DEE-spee-YOTCH-ay, mah al mo-MENT-oh noan oh TOOT-oh KWEST-oh con-TONT-ay.*
Perhaps you could mail me your bill.	*Forse può spedirmi il conto.*	*FOR-say pwoh sped-EAR-me eel CONE-toh.*
Isn't it too early to administer last rites?	*Crede sia troppo presto per l'estrema unzione?*	*CRAY-do SEE-ah TROH-poh PREST-oh pair les-TRAY-mah oon-zee-OWN-ay?*
Okay, okay, I'll pay up!	*Va bene, va bene, pagherò!*	*Vah BANE-ay, vah BANE-ay, pah-gare-OH!*
I didn't know you accepted Mastercard.	*Non sapevo che accettavate la Mastercard.*	*Noan sah-PAY-voh kay ah-CHET-ah-VOT-ay la Mastercard.*

THE SHOE AND THE WALLET

Italy is the undisputed arbiter of style in *scarpe* (footwear). Italian cobblers create shoes from the skins of an incredible variety of organisms. Colors and materials range from basic black canvas to Technicolor leather.

Dealing with shoe salespeople requires a few simple phrases.

Those crocodile loafers are really beautiful.	*Quelle pantofole di coccodrillo sono veramente stupende.*	*KWELL-ay pan-TOH-foh-lay dee COKE-oh-DREEL-oh SO-noh VAIR-ah-MENT-ay stoo-PEND-ay.*
I had better buy a pair before they're extinct.	*Meglio che ne prenda un paio prima che finiscano.*	*MAIL-yo kay nay PREND-ah oon PIE-yo PREE-mah kay fee-NEE-scah-noh.*
Do you have it in another color?	*Ne ha di un altro colore?*	*Nay ah dee oon AHL-troh coh-LORE-ay?*
The pale blue clashes with my slacks.	*Il celeste stona con i miei pantaloni.*	*Eel chay-LEST-ay STONE-ah cone ee me-AY PONT-ah-LONE-ee.*

I'll take them. By the way, how much are they?	*Le prendo. Quanto costano più o meno?*	*Lay PREND-oh. KWON-toh COAST-ah-noh pyu oh MAIN-oh.*

Fine. But let me call my banker.	*Va bene. Ma mi faccia chiamare la mia banca.*	*Vah BANE-ay. Mah me FOTCH-ah kyah-MAR-ay la MEE-ah BONK-ah.*

PRAYER TO SAINT FERRAGAMO

Oh Saint Ferragamo, Precious Cobbler to the Stars, Gifted Designer of Soles, grant me just one pair of those open-heeled high heels I saw in the window tonight, the purple ones. Size six would be perfect, Blessed Hooved One.

O San Ferragamo, Calzolaio Prezioso alle Stelle, Stilista Dotato di Suole, concedimi un paio di quelle scarpe tipo chanel a tacco alto che ho visto in vetrina questa notte, quelle bordeaux. La misura trentasei sarebbe perfetta, Siano Benedetti i Portatori di Zoccoli.

ARMANI VERSUS OUR MONEY

Italian men's clothing is at the cutting edge of fashion and price. But even if you can afford it, a good Italian suit is simply *too* stylish unless you are slim, live in Manhattan, and use mousse. People caught wearing Versace in Cincinnati usually spend the night in jail.

Nevertheless, trying on suits in a sleek little Italian shop is an entertaining way to waste a salesman's valuable time.

Wow. This is some snazzy suit.	*Wow. Questo vestito è divino.*	*Wow. KWEST-oh ves-TEET-oh ay dee-VEEN-oh.*
Could I get wider lapels?	*Posso avere i risvolti della giacca più grandi?*	*POE-soh ah-VAIR-ay ee reez-VOLT-ee DELL-ah JOCK-ah pyu GRON-dee?*
I'd like them to meet in back.	*Vorrei che si congiungessero sul dietro.*	*Vore-AY kay see kon-joon-JESS-air-oh sool dee-AY-troh.*
Ah! This duffel bag matches the suit.	*Ah! Questa sacca si intona con il vestito.*	*Ah! KWEST-ah SOCK-ah see een-TONE-ah cone eel ves-TEET-oh.*

Oh, this isn't a duffel bag. This is a pair of pants.	*Oh, non è una sacca. Sono dei pantaloni.*	*Oh, noan ay OON-ah SOCK-ah. SO-noh day PONT-ah-LONE-ee.*
I could never wear this suit in Midland.	*Non potrei mai portare questo vestito a Midland.*	*Noan poe-TRAY my por-TAH-ray KWEST-oh ves-TEET-oh ah MEED-lon.*
But I'd love to wear it around Rome.	*Ma sarebbe stupendo portarlo in giro per Roma.*	*Mah sah-RAY-bay stoo-PEND-oh por-TAR-loh in JEER-oh pair ROME-ah.*
Could I rent it?	*Posso noleggiarlo?*	*POE-soh no-lay-JAR-loh?*

SHOPPING AND SIGHT-SEEING

UNDERSTANDING ITALIAN BUSINESS HOURS

Every traveler knows that Italians keep schedules that are different from ours. The Wicked Traveler knows how they actually fill those schedules.

	What They're Doing	What's Happening to You
MORNING		
8:00	Fondling spouse.	Woken by disturbing noises.
9:00	Shooting espresso.	Woken by maid.
10:00	On the phone at work, making "lunch" plans.	Line at bank is even wider than it is long.
11:00	Discussing opposite sex with fellow employee.	Car rental clerks chatter endlessly among themselves.
12:00	Pre-lunch grooming.	Pharmacist invisible.
AFTERNOON		
1:00	Racing to arms of lover.	Museum closed for "lunch."
2:00	Consuming enormous amounts of food.	Restaurant has stopped serving.
3:00	Even more food.	Egg salad sandwich.
4:00	Cappuccino in café.	Meet charming stranger in café. Campari begins taking effect.

EVENING		
5:00	Strolling back to work.	Meet charming stranger on street.
6:00	Sweet-talking spouse by phone.	Make eyes with bartender, who is on the phone.
7:00	Changing clothes at home. Family shouting match.	Campari recharge is effective, but charming strangers are gone.
8:00	Meeting lover.	Restaurant filled with tourists.
9:00	Strolling along river.	Make eyes with charming strollers.
10:00	Quiet dinner at home.	Streets deserted.

LATE EVENING		
11:00	Fondling spouse.	Return to hotel. Odd cooing sounds from other rooms.
12:00	Retiring to separate bedroom to read.	Practice Italian for next day's adventures.
1:00	Well-earned sleep.	Well-earned sleep.

SOLVING THE RIDDLE OF MUSEUM HOURS

The museum hours published in guide books are almost totally useless. If a museum *chiude* (closes) at 1:00 P.M., it means that at 12:45 the building will be empty and the employees will already be home eating lunch. Of course, there will never be a schedule for strikes, renovations, whims, or acts of God.

Why is the museum closed today?	*Ma perché è chiuso il museo oggi?*	*Mah pair-KAY ay CUE-soh eel moo-ZAY-oh OH-jee?*
Who the hell is Saint Fiammetta?	*Chi diavolo è Santa Fiammetta?*	*Key dee-AH-voh-loh ay SAHN-tah fee-ah-MET-ah?*
One ecstatic vision and she gets a national holiday?	*Una sola visione estatica ed ha avuto un giorno festivo nazionale?*	*OON-ah SO-lah VEEZ-ee-OWN-ay ay-STOT-ee-kah aid ah ah-VOOT-oh oon JOR-noh fest-EE-voh NOTS-ee-oh-NAL-ay?*
Why is the museum closed tomorrow?	*Ma perché il museo è chiuso domani?*	*Mah pair-KAY eel moo-ZAY-oh ay CUE-soh doh-MAH-nee?*

SHOPPING AND SIGHT-SEEING

How long will they be on strike?	*Quanto tempo staranno in sciopero?*	*KWON-toh TEMP-oh star-ON-oh een SHOW-pair-oh?*
Is it true that the renovation began in 1954?	*È vero che il restauro è cominciato nel mille novecento cinquantaquattro?*	*Ay VAIR-oh kay eel rest-OW-roh ay coh-meen-CHOT-oh nell MEAL-ay NOVE-ay-CHENT-oh cheen-KWONT-ah-KWAH-troh?*
Ah, the contractor is the cardinal's nephew!	*O, l'imprenditore è il nipote del cardinale!*	*Oh, lim-PREND-ee-TORE-ay ay eel nee-POTE-ay dell car-dee-NAL-ay!*
We just want to see the Madonna.	*Vogliamo soltanto vedere la Madonna.*	*Vole-YAH-moh sole-TONT-oh vay-DARE-ay lah mah-DOAN-ah.*
Please. We're in love.	*Per favore. Siamo innamorati.*	*Pair fah-VORE-ay. See-YA-mo EEN-ah-more-AH-tee.*
Oh, thank you so much. We'll never forget you.	*O, grazie mille. Non la dimenticheremo mai.*	*Oh, GROT-zee-ay MEAL-ay. Noan lah dee-MENT-ee-care-AY-moh my.*

YOUR EMERGENCY CONFESSION

Visitors should be warned
that Italian priests are
very different from the
ones at home. But if a
confession is absolutely
necessary, there are a few
phrases worth knowing.

Forgive me father, for I have sinned.	*Mi perdoni padre, perché ho peccato.*	*Mee pair-DOAN-ee PAH-dray, pair-KAY oh pay-COT-oh.*
It has been two hours/days/ weeks/months/ years since my last confession.	*Sono passati due ore/giorni/ settimane/mesi/ anni dalla mia ultima confessione.*	*SO-noh pah-SOT-ee DOO-ay ORE-ay/JOR-nee/SET-ee-MON-ay/MAY-zee/ON-ee DAH-lah MEE-ah OOL-teem-ah con-FESS-ee-OWN-ay.*
I've made love to six women/ men since my arrival.	*Dal mio arrivo ho fatto l'amore con sei donne/ uomini.*	*Doll MEE-oh ah-REEV-oh oh FAH-toh lah-MORE-ay cone SAY DOAN-ay/ WHOA-me-nee.*
Yesterday.	*Ieri.*	*Ee-AIR-ee.*

RELIGION, POLITICS, AND SPORTS

I didn't come here to be congratulated, father.	*Non sono venuto qui per ricevere delle congratulazioni, padre.*	*Noan SO-noh vay-NOOT-oh kwee pair ree-CHAY-vair-ay DELL-ay con-GRAH-too-LOT-zee-OWN-ay, PAH-dray.*
Two Hail Marys is a little light, don't you think?	*Due Ave Marie sono un po' poco, non crede?*	*DOO-ay AH-vay mah-REE-ay SO-noh oon poh POH-coh, noan CRAY-day?*
How about a couple of Our Fathers, too?	*Piuttosto due Padre Nostri?*	*Pyu TOAST-oh DOO-ay PAH-dray NO-stree?*
Thank you, father.	*Grazie, padre.*	*GROT-zee-ay, PAH-dray.*
But I'm busy this evening.	*Ma sono impegnato questa sera.*	*Mah SO-noh EEM-pain-YOT-oh KWEST-ah SAIR-ah.*
Is tomorrow night good?	*Domani sera andrebbe bene?*	*Doh-MON-ee SAIR-ah on-DRAY-bay BANE-ay?*
About eight then?	*Alle otto allora?*	*AH-lay OAT-oh ah-LORE-ah?*

POLITICAL DISCOURSE

It's usually best to avoid sharing political views in countries where people take these things seriously. Fortunately for those who can't keep their mouths shut, Italian politics aren't taken seriously by anyone.

Italian politicians hold office so briefly that including names here would be pointless. Instead, general comments are provided.

I love Italian politics!	*Adoro la politica italiana!*	*Ah-DOOR-oh lah poh-LEE-tee-cah ee-tal-YON-ah!*
Fifty-eight governments since World War II!	*Cinquantotto governi dalla seconda guerra mondiale!*	*CHEEN-kwan-TOTE-oh go-VAIR-nee DAH-lah say-CONE-dah GWARE-ah moan-dee-AH-lay!*
Cardinals and gangsters vying for politcal power!	*Cardinali e gangster che si contendono il potere politico!*	*Car-dee-NAL-ee ay GANG-stair kay see cone-tend-oh-noh eel poh-TARE-ay poh-LEE-tee-co!*
Porno queens in parliament! Great!	*E stelle del porno in parlamento! Fantastico!*	*Ay STELL-ay dell PORN-oh een PAR-lah-MENT-oh! Fon-TOST-tee-coh!*

RELIGION, POLITICS, AND SPORTS

Workers and intellectuals in the same party!	*Operai e intellettuali negli stessi partiti!*	*OPE-air-eye ay EEN-tay-LEH-too-AH-lay AHL-yee STESS-ee por-TEE-tee!*
Just like the old days in my country!	*Proprio come ai miei tempi!*	*PRO-pree-oh COH-may eye mee-AY TEMP-ee!*
The Italian political system is the world's fairest.	*Il sistema politico italiano è il più democratico del mondo.*	*Eel sees-TAME-ah poh-LEE-tee-coh ee-tal-YON-oh ay eel pyu day-moh-CROT-ee-coh del MOAN-doh.*
Sooner or later everyone gets to be president, for fifteen minutes.	*Tutti prima o poi fanno il presidente, per quindici minuti.*	*TOOT-ee PREE-mah oh poy FAH-noh eel prez-ee-DENT-ee, pair KWEEN-deetch-ee mee-NOOT-ee.*

RELIGION, POLITICS, AND SPORTS

AUTHENTIC SCREAMING FOR SPECTATORS

Italians hate to die on Saturday, because it means they have to miss Sunday's *calcio* (soccer) match.

Calcio enthusiasts are loud and obscene, but Italian fans are, by international standards, restrained. They kill fewer than a dozen of their fellows each season.

Visitors who wish to understand what is being shouted at a *calcio* match should study the following phrases.

To players of the opposition:

You sissy!	*Frocio!*	*FROH-choh!*
Go home to Mommy!	*Tornatene dalla mammina!*	*TORN-ah-TAY-nay DAH-lah mah-MEAN-ah!*
You play like an old dog!	*Giochi da cane vecchio!*	*JOKE-ee dah CON-ay VECK-ee-oh!*

To the home team:

Into the mouth of the wolf!	*In bocca al lupo!*	*Een BOKE-ah al LOOP-oh!*
May the wolf die!	*Crepi il lupo!*	*CRAY-pee eel LOOP-oh!*

🏛 RELIGION, POLITICS, AND SPORTS

Up the ass of the whale!	*In culo alla balena!*	*Een COOL-oh AH-lah bah-LAIN-ah!*
Hope he doesn't fart!	*Speriamo che non scoreggi!*	*SPARE-ee-YOM-oh kay noan score-EDGE-ee!*

To the referees:

Blockhead!	*Sei di tek!*	*Say dee tek!*
Traitor!	*Traditore!*	*Trah-dee-TORE-ay!*
Get some glasses!	*Mettiti un paio di occhiali!*	*Meh-TEE-tee oon PIE-oh dee OAK-ee-AHL-ee!*
Snake!	*Serpente!*	*Sair-PENT-ay!*
Whose payroll are you on?	*Ma chi t'ha pagato?*	*Mah key tah pah-GOT-oh?*

MEN: UNLEASH THE LATIN LOVER INSIDE YOU

To compete with the natives, non-European men must know two things: Italian men are willing to exaggerate beyond all the bounds of reason, and women are willing to believe them.

Sometimes.

I have never known love until now.	*Non ho mai conosciuto l'amore fino ad oggi.*	*Noan oh my CONE-oh- SHOOT-oh la- MORE-ay FEEN-oh odd OH-jee.*
The profound mystery of whatever you just said sets my heart on fire.	*Il profondo mistero di ciò che stai dicendo mi infuoca il cuore.*	*Eel pro-FOND-oh mee-STAIR-oh dee cho kay sty dee-CHEND-oh me een-FWOKE-ah eel KWORE-ay.*
I will kill myself if you ever leave me.	*Se mi lasci mi uccido.*	*Say mee LOSH-ee mee oo-CHEE-doh.*
What is your name, my celestial fruit basket?	*Come ti chiami, mio cestino di frutta celestiale?*	*COH-may tee KYAH-mee, MEE-oh chess-TEEN-oh dee FROOT-ah chay-LESS-tee-AL-ay?*

Your name is like an ageless aria to my ears.	*Il tuo nome suona alle mie orecchie come una melodia senza età.*	*Eel TOO-oh NOH-may SWONE-ah AH-lay MEE-ay oh-RECK-ee-ay COH-may OON-ah may-loh-DEE-yah SEN-sah ay-TAH.*
What? This man is your husband!?	*Che cosa? Quello è tuo marito!?*	*Kay COZE-ah? KWELL-oh ay TOO-oh mah-REET-oh!?*
You deserve greater joy than such a man could ever provide!	*Meriti ben altra gioia che quella che può dare un tipo così!*	*MARE-ee-tee bane AHL-trah JOY-ah kay KWELL-ah kay pwoh DAR-ay oon TEEP-oh coh-SEE.*
You deny our everlasting love!?	*Neghi l'amore eterno!?*	*NEG-ee lah-MORE-ay ay-TAIRN-oh!?*
Then at least give me your phone number, my heavenly marinara sauce.	*Almeno dammi il tuo numero di telefono, mio sugo alla marinara.*	*Ahl-MAIN-oh DAH-mee eel TOO-oh NOOM-air-oh dee tay-LAY-foh-noh, MEE-oh SOOG-oh AH-lah MAR-ee-NAR-ah.*

WOMEN: DEFLATE THE LATIN LOVER BEHIND YOU

An Italian man is unlikely to be dangerous in daylight, but he might act like a caveman in front of (or behind) women he doesn't know personally, particularly those in shorts. The wise female visitor arms herself with a few appropriate phrases, a spine-tingling scream, and a large pair of scissors.

Don't touch me.	*Non mi tocchi.*	*Noan mee TOKE-ee.*
Buzz off, garlic breath.	*Vada via che sa di aglio.*	*VAH-da VEE-ah kay sah dee AHL-yoh.*
You're disgusting.	*Fa schifo.*	*Fah SKEE-foh.*
The Sicilian sun has cooked your brain.	*Il sole siciliano le ha cotto il cervello.*	*Eel SOLE-ay see-cheel-YON-oh lay hah COAT-oh eel chair-VELL-oh.*
Not if you were the last man on earth.	*Neanche se lei fosse l'unico uomo sulla terra.*	*Nay-ONK-ay say lay FOSS-ay LOON-ee-coh WHOA-moh SOO-lah TAIR-ah.*
Filth!	*Sporco!*	*SPORE-coh!*

Leave me alone.	*Mi lasci in pace.*	*Mee LOSH-ee in POTCH-ay.*
You've got a lot of class. Working class.	*Lei ha molta classe. Classe proletaria.*	*Lay ah MOLE-tah KLOSS-ay. KLOSS-ay PRO-leh-TAR-ee-ah.*
I'll call the police.	*Chiamo la polizia.*	*KYAH-moh lah poh-leet-SEE-ah.*
Help!	*Aiuto!*	*Eye-YOU-toh!*

PET NAMES: ANIMAL

A few good *vezzeggiativi* (pet names) add authenticity to an *avventúra* (love affair).

Kitten	*Micio*	*MEECH-oh*
Bunny	*Coniglietto*	*CON-eel-YET-oh*
Duckling	*Paperella**	*PAP-air-ELL-ah*
Little Sparrow	*Passerotto*	*POSS-air-OAT-oh*
Little Mouse	*Topolino*	*TOPE-oh-LEEN-oh*
Little Squirrel	*Scoiattolino*	*skoy-OTT-oh-LEEN-oh*

*refers to women only

MAKING LOVE

The following phrases
are provided for the man
who wishes to master
them, and for the woman
who wishes to recognize them.

You look beautiful in the candlelight.	*Sei bella al lume di candela.*	*Say BELL-ah AH-lah LOO-may dee con-DEL-ah.*
You must be even more beautiful in the dark.	*Devi essere più bella nell'oscurità.*	*DAY-vee ESS-air-ay pyu BELL-ah nell oh-SKOOR-ee-TAH.*
Would you like a Campari/some Chianti?	*Gradisci un Campari/ Chianti?*	*Gra-DEESH-ee oon com-PAR-ee/ kee-YONT-ee?*
Will you join me for dinner?	*Verresti a cena con me?*	*Vay-REST-ee ah CHAIN-ah cone may?*
My wife is very fat, and has many warts.	*Mia moglie e grassissima ed è piena di porri.*	*MEE-ah MOLE-yay ay gra-SEES-ee-mah aid ay pee-EN-ah dee PORR-ee.*
She no longer loves me.	*Non mi ama più.*	*Noan mee AH-mah pyu.*

PET NAMES: VEGETABLE

Little Sugar	*Zuccherino*	*ZOOK-air-EEN-oh*
Little Sweetie	*Dolcezza*	*dole-CHETS-ah*
Little Cookie	*Biscottino*	*BEESK-oh-TEEN-oh*
Little Strawberry	*Fragolina**	*FROG-oh-LEAN-ah*

*refers to women only

Dinner was delicious. What's for dessert?	*La cena era squisita. Cosa c'è per dessert?*	*Lah CHAIN-ah AIR-ah SQUEEZE-ee-tah. COZE-ah chay pair dess-AIRT?*
Would you like to see my sculptures?	*Ti piacerebbe vedere le mie sculture?*	*Tee pee-OTCH-air-ABE-ay vay-DARE-ay lay MEE-ay skool-TURE-ay?*
May I show you my obelisk?	*Posso mostrarti il mio obelisco?*	*POE-soh moh-STRAR-tee eel MEE-oh OH-bay-LEES-coh?*
Take off your clothes.	*Spogliati.*	*SPOLE-yah-tee.*

(CONTINUED)

THOSE FRIENDLY ITALIANS ♥

Take off my clothes.	*Spogliami.*	*SPOLE-yah-mee.*
You are very beautiful.	*Sei molto bella.*	*Say MOLE-toh BELL-ah.*
Your breasts are like melons from Tuscany.	*Il tuo seno è come i meloni toscani.*	*Eel TOO-oh SANE-oh ay COH-may ee may-LONE-ee toe-SKAH-nee.*
Hug me.	*Abbracciami.*	*Ah-BROTCH-ah-mee.*
Kiss me.	*Baciami.*	*BOTCH-ah-mee.*
My treasure.	*Tesoro mio.*	*Tay-ZORE-oh MEE-oh.*
Slower.	*Più piano.*	*Pyu pee-AH-noh.*
Faster.	*Più in fretta.*	*Pyu een FRETT-ah.*
Oh my God.	*Oh mio Dio.*	*Oh MEE-oh DEE-oh.*
I love you.	*Ti amo.*	*Tee ah-moh.*
I will never leave you.	*Non ti lascerò mai.*	*Noan tee LOSH-air-OH my.*

DENYING YOUR INFIDELITY

Italians are naturally suspicious of their lovers. Any tourist lucky enough to get embroiled in Italian romance will need a few bold-faced lies.

Here are some flowers.	*Ecco dei fiori.*	*ECK-oh day fee-ORE-ee.*
Sorry I'm late.	*Scusa il ritardo.*	*SCOO-sah eel ree-TARD-oh.*
But I love only you, my sweet.	*Ma amo solo te, dolcezza mia.*	*Mah AH-moh SO-loh tay, dole-CHETS-ah-MEE-ah.*
What are you talking about?	*Che stai dicendo?*	*Kay sty dee-CHEND-oh?*
Her/Him? Don't make me laugh.	*Lei/Lui? Ma non mi far ridere.*	*LAY/LOO-ee? Mah noan mee far REED-air-ay.*
I could never love a woman/man like her/him.	*Non potrei mai amare una donna/un uomo come lei/lui.*	*Noan po-TRAY my ah-MAR-ay OON-ah DOAN-ah/oon WHOA-moh COH-may LAY/LOO-ee.*
She/He is twenty years younger/older than I am!	*Ha vent'anni meno/più di me!*	*Ah vain-TAH-nee MAY-noh/pyu dee may!*

(CONTINUED)

THOSE FRIENDLY ITALIANS

Her breasts are much too large for my taste.	*Le sue tette sono troppo grandi per i miei gusti.*	*Lay SOO-ay TET-ay SO-noh TROH-poh GRON-dee, pair ee mee-AY GOOSE-tee.*
You know I don't like macho men.	*Lo sai che non mi piacciono i maschioni.*	*Loh sigh kay noan mee pee-OTCH-oh-noh ee MASK-ee-OWN-ee.*
Besides, she/he is married.	*Per di più è sposato/a.*	*Pair dee pyu ay spo-ZOT-oh/ah.*
You're imagining things.	*Tu sogni.*	*Too SOAN-yee.*

PET NAMES: CELESTIAL

My Soul	***Anima Mia***	*ON-ee-mah MEE-ah*
My Love	***Amore Mio***	*ah-MORE-ay MEE-oh*
Treasure	***Tesoro***	*tay-ZORE-oh*
Angel	***Angelo***	*ON-jell-oh*

EFFECTIVE LETTER-WRITING

Seasoned tourists always send *biglietti di grazie* (thank-you notes) to their hosts and drop cards to people they meet during their adventures. These are the travelers who are invited to stay in the homes of natives. They have richer cultural experiences and lower hotel bills.

Letters and cards are more effective when the author makes a sincere attempt to use the native language. The following are phrases commonly needed in this type of correspondence.

Dear John/Martha,	*Caro/a Giovanni/Martina,*
It was a great pleasure to meet you.	*È stato un vero piacere incontrarti.*
Your entire family is wonderful.	*Tutta la tua famiglia è fantastica.*
I've never heard so much shouting!	*Non ho mai sentito urlare così tanto!*
I admire the Italian passion for debate.	*Ammiro la passione italiana per le discussioni.*
Sorry about the tomato sauce episode.	*Mi dispiace per l'incidente della pommarola.*
I hope the stains came out.	*Spero che le macchie siano venute via.*

(CONTINUED)

THOSE FRIENDLY ITALIANS

That grappa was the smoothest rocket fuel I've ever tasted.	*Quella grappa era il carburante più morbido che abbia mai assaggiato.*
Sorry if my pope jokes offended anyone.	*Scusami, se il mio scherzo sul papa ha offeso qualcuno.*
I admit that the one about the blind virgin was in poor taste.	*Ammetto che quello sulla vergine cieca era di cattivo gusto.*
Sorry about your parents/spouse catching us in the act.	*Mi dispiace che i tuoi genitori/tuo marito ci abbiano/ci abbia sorpreso sul più bello.*
By the way, I don't believe the baby is mine/you'll soon be a father.	*A proposito, non credo che il bambino sia mio/presto sarai padre.*
I miss you very much.	*Ma è finita tra di noi.*
But it's over between us.	*Ma è finito tra di noi.*
Yours truly, (Your name)	*Caramente, (Your name)*